CW00859343

I

Poetry is when an
emotion has found it's
thought and the thought
has found words.

~ Robert Frost ~

978-1-387-47720-3 Imprint: Lulu.com

Wisdom Lines

BY

PAULA PATRICE

THIS PROJECT IS DEDICATED

TO TABITHA BOOTH,

MY TALENTED, CREATIVE GRANDDAUGHTER. WHEN I SPOKE OF THE (WELL EARNED) WRINKLES ON MY FACE, SHE SAID "GRAMMY, THEY ARE WISDOM LINES".

TO PAUL BOOTH,

MY MOST CREATIVE, TALENTED SON, WHO ENCOURAGED AND INSPIRED ME TO COMPILE MY COLLECTION OF POEMS, AND WHO FORMATTED AND PRODUCED THESE WORKS.

TO PAOLA DURAN

MY SOURCE OF SUPPORT AND ENCOURAGEMENT WHO USED HER TALENT AS AN ACCOMPLISHED PHOTOGRAPHER TO ARRANGE THE PHOTOGRAPHY.

TO LYNDA VEECH

MY DEAR, SWEET AND TALENTED NIECE WHO IS AN EXTRAORDINARY MUSICIAN AND MUSIC EDUCATOR, EDITED THESE WORKS.

IT IS WITH PLEASURE THAT I SHARE MY "WISDOM" DEVELOPED OVER THE DECADES.

INTRODUCTION

1957 - 2020

OVER MANY DECADES, I WROTE AS A METHOD OF EXPRESSING MY THOUGHTS. BEING RAISED IN AN ITALIAN, CATHOLIC CULTURE, I HAD VERY DEFINED BOUNDARIES AND GUIDELINES. WE LEARNED BY BEING OBEDIENT, LISTENING, WATCHING AND HOPING WE GOT THINGS RIGHT.

THE RULE WAS TO DO WHAT WAS "RIGHT" AND TO NEVER COMPROMISE THE FAMILY NAME IN ANY WAY. ONE'S QUESTIONS AND CONCERNS REGARDING WHAT TO EXPECT IN LIFE WAS WRAPPED IN THE "RULES".

OUR ENVIRONMENT REFLECTED A PROTECTED LIFE BOUND BY FAMILY, RELIGIOUS, EDUCATIONAL AND CULTURAL EXPECTATIONS.

THROUGH THESE TIMES, WE GREW, WE THRIVED AND WE FOUND OUR WAY TO COPE AND FIND HAPPINESS.

MAY YOU ALSO FIND YOUR WAY.

FORWARD

1980 – 2020

"Discretion … the better part of valor!"

A cliché that causes society to be more comfortable with actions that reflect traditional and religious mores.

Although the guidelines to personal and sexual relationships have become less clear-cut, there is a strong vein running through our society that maintains a rather delicate balance of morality.

One's life experiences, successes and failures will determine what one considers right or wrong, good or bad.

It is upon this base that one will choose to play the role of the "dutiful" or contrary person, or to be one who will choose to think and to reason and to choose the freedom to fly.

I have chosen the latter after much careful and ongoing deliberation. Among joys and sorrows, sadness and tears, anxieties and fears, I made a respectful decision to embrace my free thought.

I choose to enjoy each moment, each day – to pick the flowers as I walk through the garden of life; but most importantly, to feel the very essence of love, nature and the mix of wonders that life has to offer.

All of this. untarnished by the impositions of society in its attempt to capture the human spirit.

It is to the many people who feel as I do, and to those who wish they could, that I address my thoughts on life, love and the complexities of the human spirit.

It is with hope that these thoughts may awaken one's sense of self, embellish the desire to deal with one's adversities and to seek out the joys of life…

if only for today and tomorrow, as each forever may never be known.

By Paula Patrice

TRIED AND TRUE "ISMS" ... FROM MANY SOURCES

TO HELP ONE MAKE SENSE OF ONE'S JOURNEY

1. LIFT THE VAIL OF SELF-DOUBT. YOU ARE WORTHY TO LOVE YOURSELF.

2. BE THE CONFIDENT PERSON YOU CAN BE.

3. GET TO KNOW YOURSELF AND BE PROUD OF WHO YOU ARE.

4. BECAUSE SOMEONE ELSE "LIKES", DOES NOT MEAN THAT YOU MUST ALSO.

5. STAND FIRM ON WHO YOU ARE AND WHAT YOU LIKE. YOU CAN STILL RESPECT ANOTHER'S VIEW WITHOUT OFFENDING THEM.

6. BE MINDFUL OF YOUR DECISIONS AS THE IMPACT WILL CONTINUE TO BE PART OF YOUR LIFE.

7. ONLY YOU CAN MAKE A MEANINGFUL DECISION FOR YOU ... FOR YOU ONLY, WALK IN YOUR SHOES.

8. WHEN THINGS GO WRONG, USE IT AS A LEARNING TOOL TO IMPROVE YOURSELF.

9. IF A DECISION IS NOT GOOD FOR YOU, DO NOT REPEAT IT AGAIN. GROW FROM IT.

10. LOVE THE PEOPLE WHO CARE ABOUT YOU WITHOUT COERCION ... THAT IS A TREASURE.

VIII

Table of Contents

Decision
1957

Each Path ... a tangent unknown.
A road which no one can be shown.
Far too many have been through
that path so new to you.

The big decision you must make,
decide which road you ought to take.
Take each step with firm conviction
and utmost faith in your decision.

Your cycle soon will grow too stagnant,
unless you veer off on your tangent.
So do not hesitate to chance,
your life each day you must enhance.

You reach a dead end when you blunder.
Detour! Do not go asunder.
Go here or there but do not stray.
Your "will", if firm, will find the way.

Dedication
1960

Love is a wondrous thing.
So often tried though true.
Love 'til your heart would sing,
Don't despair when made to be blue.

Just know there is always "I love you"
In matters that breed dismay.
Be mindful of what each may do ...
Be the dawn of each new day.

PANGS OF LOVE

1960

ONE CANNOT LIVE WITHOUT LOVE.

LOVE CANNOT LIVE WITHOUT TRUST.

TRUST WILL NOT GROW WITHOUT TRUTH.

TRUTH WILL NE'ER BE WITHOUT FAITH.

Bitterness No More

1961

Discard that shell of bitterness,
Time makes life seem kind.
Why should I wallow in loneliness
When it's all a matter of mind?

Consider life as one big game.
You sometimes win, and sometimes lose
Emerging as sad, happy, bitter, the same...
For consolation, I muse.

PRETENSE OF LIFE

1960

SOME DAYS SLIP SLOWLY BY,

YET, TIME RIPPLES QUICKLY ALONG.

AS SO MANY WONDER WHY

SO OFTEN SO MUCH IS WRONG.

PONDER ON WHAT CAN BE DONE,

THINK OF RESULTS IN DREAD.

FOR ONCE THE CYCLE IS SPUN,

IT CONTINUES UNTIL YOU ARE DEAD.

LIFE IS A SORROWFUL PITFALL,

AS ONWARD WE TREAD TOWARD OUR END;

AWAITING THE TIME OF OUR CALL,

OR WHEN OUR SAD LIFE WILL MEND.

WHAT PURPOSE CAN WE SAY?

WHAT WORTH IS THERE TO LIFE?

DEPRESSED BE NOT, PRETEND YOU'RE GAY,

PRETEND THERE IS NO STRIFE.

SOLITUDE

1961

A SERENE, SOMBER MOOD CREEPS UP SO SUDDENLY

IN AN ATMOSPHERE OF LONELY SOLITUDE.

I WONDER WHY THIS SHOULD PREVAIL?

WHY SHOULD EMOTIONS DETERMINE WHAT IS REAL?

LONELINESS AND SOLITUDE IS ALL THAT I FEEL.

BUT HOW CAN A PERSON BE LONELY AND BLUE

WHEN PART OF A CROWD OR WITH ONLY A FEW?

I TRY TO PROJECT A VIVACIOUSNESS, TRUE.

YET SOMEHOW THIS FEELING CREEPS CONSTANTLY THROUGH.

I MUST BE ON GUARD, TO BE UNPERCEIVED

BY OTHERS WHO ALSO TRY TO DECEIVE.

THAT CAREFREE APPEARANCE I TRY TO ACHIEVE

RESULTS IN A SERENE AND SOMBERLY MOOD,

THAT EATS AT MY HEART BEHIND MY WALL OF LONELY SOLITUDE.

Unbounded
1962

I need to feel free, to fly untamed.

Never surround me, it makes me feel maimed.

I adore the sensation of bigness and space,

a powerful feeling no one can erase.

Over many a mile and afar I'll speed,

and never a care or woe I'll heed.

But when one day I begin to tarry,

only then will my Prince I marry.

Through the Decades of Life
(A Tribute to my brother John – 40th Birthday)

Time is but a fleeting thing, it quickly passes by.

Settle and reflect a bit for back in time we'll fly …

You started as a babe in arms, but soon
you were a toddler,

You went to school and with your charms,
your grades you learned to barter.

As you grew, you learned a lot,
you were a "model" child,

But just so you'd not fill that slot,
at times you acted wild.

You lickety-split right through your teens,
your twenties were not sickly,

'Cause the Navy took up all your time,
you grew up pretty quickly.

You settled into life's routine,
you married and had children.

MIND OVER EMOTION
1962

ONCE MORE AS I SIT DOWN TO THINK,
I WRITE MY TALE OF WOE.
'TIS SAD THAT MAN'S WEAK NATURE REIGNS
'TIL REASON DEEMS NOT SO.

I'VE THOUGHT ABOUT THIS QUESTION,
I KNOW OF WHAT I SPEAK.
HOW FOOLISH TO HEED EMOTION
TO BE TENDER AND SO WEAK.

THROUGH EXPERIENCE YOU WILL KNOW,
TO NOT BE THE TARGET FOR HURT.
IS THERE NOT WORTH IN THE RATIONAL MIND
PROTECTING ONE FROM STRIFE?

SAD MEMORY

1962

His memory lingers on...

In one fleeting instant all of the

joys, love, anxiety comes rushing back.

It was our own.

This love which first I shunned,
feared and then accepted.

A bad decision left me dangling
somewhere between

the security and dishevelment of love.

My sadness milds with time ...
but the taste remains ...

a remnant of a love that could never be

sears through my heart like a blade

and leaves me sad but smart.

ALONE

1962

I'VE FELT THIS HURT BEFORE.

THE PAIN OF A BREAK UP!

A DEEP PAIN WITHIN MY HEART THAT LEAVES ME RESTLESS

AS I THRIVE ON SELF-PITY ONCE MORE.

MY VERY SOUL IS SO UNHAPPY

WITH EACH PASSING HOUR OF THE DAY ...

YET, WHY DO I ALLOW MY LIFE TO FILL
WITH DISAPPOINTMENT?

THERE IS TOO MUCH OF TEARS AND SORROW.

THIS LONELINESS BRINGS ME SUCH SADNESS.

IN VAIN I TAKE A WALK TO PONDER ON WHAT I MUST DO
TO MAKE LIFE SEEM WORTHWHILE.

I ASK ... DO I TRULY DEPEND ON ANOTHER'S LOVE
TO FIND THE HAPPINESS I SEEK?

I KNOW IN MY HEART THAT I MUST
RISE ABOVE THIS CONFLICT.

I CANNOT REST WITH THE THOUGHT
THAT "FATE" IS THE CULPRIT...

WHEN I FIRMLY BELIEVE THAT

WE MANAGE OUR OWN "FATE".

MASTER OF MY FATE
1962

NO ONE CAN DECIDE FOR ME
THE THOUGHT, "IS LIFE WORTHWHILE"?
NOR CAN ONE, WHEN I AM BLUE,
CONJURE ME TO SMILE.

A MELANCHOLY MOOD TRANSPIRES
DESPAIR AND DISCONTENT,
AND DEEP WITHIN MY HEART, A PAIN
TOO BITTER TO RELENT.

WHO CAN KNOW THE TEARS I'VE WEPT
THROUGH MANY DAYS I'VE KNOWN?
LORD ONLY KNOWS MY FLESH GROWS COLD
WHEN I SIT ALL ALONE.

THE RAY OF HOPE I TRY TO GRASP
BEFORE IT IS TOO LATE,
LEAVES THE REALIZATION THAT
I'M MASTER OF MY FATE.

Priceless Jewel
1962

Grasp the jewel, there it glistens,
tarnish be there naught.
Reach 'afore the glitter darkens
or ne'er again be sought.

Cast aside with chide and scorn,
glimmer feigns a glow.
Lingers on yet so forlorn
pleading to bestow.

When it be gone then all are sad,
no finer jewel uncovered.
Beauty reigneth to be had
it's secret undiscovered.

If it dims, ne'er let it darken,
succumb not to all strife.
Blossom and burst forth a 'sudden

Priceless jewel ... LIFE !

LIFE
1963

TO SEE ...

THE BEAUTY OF A ROSE ...

THE BUBBLING BROOK OR ROLLING SEA ...

THE DAWN OF EACH NEW DAY.

THAT'S WHAT LIFE IS TO ME ...

AND TO KNOW THAT THERE ARE THOSE WHO CARE

IS WHAT MAKES THAT LIFE WORTH LIVING.

Midnight Thought
(For My Very Sad Friend)
1979

There is an anxious quiver, like one about to take flight

But ... it is sadness.

A sick anxious feeling that makes life near immobile ...

The difficulty of coping ...

The drain of burdens ...

The strain on the mind and in the heart
of doing what must be done.

However ...

Have courage! Stand firm.

Have confidence! Continue onward.

Have competence and strength!
The strength to make it through.

That faint glimmer will grow as paths widen and branch ...

And through fortitude, it will happen.

But ...

Now, right now, emotions may be spent, energy may wain ...

Right now, a weary sadness prevails.

A feeling of aloneness ... but never to be alone.

For here is your friend who helps to see
the glimmer that cannot be seen alone.

A spirit to be rekindled by an understanding friend –

As the enchantment of the midnight fires
that come aglow through the ashen coals ...

So will your spirit prevail.

Be well my friend.

Fond Memories

1980

The memories we share ...

The happy times we've known ...

Will be a thing we shall cherish.

The tides ebb and flow as time itself and leaves its mark,

wearing away the shoreline
as does time wear away our sadness and hurts.

Our memories will linger as the faintness
of a long worn fragrance ...

And the pain of parting will have become like a

sea shell rushed back by the waves of a storm

then ...

deeply buried by "two" in the sands.

When they searched it could not be found again,

for it lay preserved in the quietness of the dunes ...

just beyond their reach.

World of Poetry Honorable Mention - 1986

GIVE LOVE A CHANCE

1980

LET ME KNOW YOU. LET ME REALLY KNOW YOU.

LET ME INTO YOUR LIFE ...
LET ME SHARE YOUR FEARS AND SORROWS.

LET ME INTO YOUR HEART ...

LET ME LOVE YOU AND YOU LOVE ME.

DON'T BE AFRAID, I'D NEVER HURT YOU.

BE OPEN, HONEST AND TRUE.

DON'T BREAKUP OUR HEARTS IF YOU LOVE ME,

LET IT HAPPEN AND WE COULD BE FREE.

Sea Scene
1980

I watch the seagulls soar ...
Mystified by their grace and ease in flight;

But they are restless to be fed.
I hear the cries and chatter of those about me

slip into the sound of the waves that peak and
crash into the shore.
And I am mesmerized by the roll and rhythm of the sea
nudging relentlessly against the jetty.

I feel the sand blowing gently against my skin
as the heat of the sun penetrates to my bones.

And I enjoy the comfort of an understanding silence
from my friend who sits quietly beside me.

As the hours pass me by, the moments seem so few ...
The tide comes in to touch my toes, reality comes too,
as the seagulls fly away ...

To Capture a Moment
1980

Perched atop a stump on the jetty,
overcome by the beauty of the sea,

looking over the waters ...
Following the shoreline
until it disappears into the horizon.

Thousands of ripples
nestle onto the shoreline and disappear.
The tide is low,
its fingers reaching out to embrace the land ...

A never-ending, mystifying
happening, of which I never tire ...

The wind blows, the sun sets, and I?
I sit alone in peace, as one with the gentle sea.

Tranquility

The sun ...

The sea ...

Sun and Sea Fantasy

1980

The sun glistening on the choppy ripples in the sea

cuts a silver path into the blue horizon ...

sparkling like a million twinkling stars.

Wishing I could but prance along
that path into the far beyond

that stretches on ...

Sparkling, inviting, little twinkling stars.

The rise and fall of the rolling waves
is like a rocking horse in motion ...

Sparkling, playful, little twinkling stars.

Alas! Our boat turns off my silver path
that reaches across the ocean

and suddenly there are no more ...

No twinkling little stars.

FLEETING MOMENT

1981

I WONDER WHERE MY LIFE WILL LEAD?
I PONDER WHERE IT WILL GO ...
SOMETIMES I HAVE A HANDLE ON IT
YET, TIMES I JUST DON'T KNOW.

DREAM ON ...

1981

I OFTEN WONDER ABOUT YOU AND ME.

I WISH I COULD SOMEHOW KNOW ...

WILL OUR LIVES TOGETHER BE?

WE SAY THAT IT COULD BE SO!

THE MANY YEARS PAST HAVE GONE VERY SWIFTLY

AS WE THINK IN RETROSPECT.

THE NEXT FEW YEARS COULD GO SLOWLY,

IT WILL TELL THE TALE I EXPECT.

WE'VE COME A VERY LONG WAY FROM THE START,

MORE THAN WE'D DARE EVER DREAM.

IT'S HARD TO CONCEIVE THAT WE EVER WOULD PART

THERE'S NO DOUBT WE'RE A WINNING TEAM.

MY "LIL BRO"

2020

I HAVE A LITTLE BROTHER,

OF HIM I TOOK GREAT CARE.

ALONG THE WAY I MADE A POINT TO TEACH HIM HOW TO SHARE.

I'M PROUD OF HOW HE'S GROWN TO HAVE SO MUCH INTEGRITY.

HE'S KIND, TAKES PRIDE,

AND YET HE IS AS HUMBLE AS CAN BE.

MY "LIL BRO", GOOD NATURED,

HIS READY SMILE FOUND.

HE'S ALWAYS WITH A HELPING HAND,

A JOY TO HAVE AROUND.

Thoughts on Divorce

1981

Sometimes you are in a situation that is so uncomfortable for you

that you will have to leave so that you can survive.

You find you must leave the physical set-up,

not necessarily leave the children.

A parent can leave a marriage
but one does not divorce a child.

Arrangements are made.

It is the child's right to see an absent parent,

and the parent's responsibility to care for the child.

When you get to the point when you have had enough,

You will leave all, and do what must be done.

The Power of Love
1982

Our love is likened to the spring after the frost,
the calm after the storm,
ashen coals that come aglow.

Our love would make the silent birds sing,
the hidden sun shine,
the tides ebb and flow.

Our love will transcend all obstacles and woe,
and through but the days ahead,
our love will continue to grow.

Then one joyous day we will be together,
for a love like ours
is rare and forever.

CHALLENGE OF THE WIND

1981

THE WIND WHISTLES GENTLY THROUGH THE TREES ...
ALL ELSE IS QUIET ...

EXCEPT FOR THAT WIND SINGING ITS TUNE.
IF I COULD NOT HEAR ITS SONG, I COULD STILL SEE THE TREES

BENDING AND SWAYING UNDER ITS WILL ...
ALL IS NOT WELL, FOR THE WIND GREW IMPOSING AND FIERCE,

CREATING TURMOIL THAT INCREASED IN WAVES
THAT EBBED AND FLOWED.

THOSE TREES THAT BENT AND SWAYED STOOD FIRM
IN THE AFTERMATH OF THE ANGERED WIND.

THOSE LACKING ELASTICITY SURELY SNAP ...
AND THE SHEAR OF THE WOODSMAN'S BLADE TOOK COMMAND.

UNTIL WE MEET AGAIN ...

(GOODBYE TO A DEAR FRIEND)

1981

WE'VE GROWN TOGETHER THROUGH THE YEARS ...

NOW TIME HAS COME TO PART.

WHO CAN EVER PUT INTO WORDS,

WHAT IS FELT WITHIN EACH HEART?

I'LL NOT SAY GOODBYE, NOR BID THEE ADIEU.

FARE – THEE – WELL IS MY WISH FOR YOU ...

FOR MY LOVE GOES TO REST WITH YOU.

LEAVES OF MANY COLORS
1981

THE WIND BLOWS ... AT TIMES MORE VIOLENTLY THAN OTHERS,

AND THE LEAVES OF MANY COLORS, BLOW HITHER AND YON.

THE SPIRIT OF THE WIND IS RESTLESS ...

IT SCATTERS THE NESTLING LEAVES.

THEY SETTLE FOR ONLY A MOMENT AND BLOW ON AND FAR AWAY.

RARELY DO THEY RETURN,

ALWAYS ONWARD AND OUTWARD,

ALL TIMES WITH NO DIRECTION.

UNTIL ...

ONE MAY REST GENTLY AGAINST A ROCK WHERE IT MAY STILL
TAKE FLIGHT.

SHOULD IT CATCH UPON A FENCE IT MAY BE TORN APART.

SOME OF IT REMAINS AS DUST UPON THE EARTH,

YET, SOME CONTINUES ONWARD AND SCATTERS IN THE WIND.

THOUGH NOW IN DIFFERENT FORM, STILL FREE TO FLY AWAY,

THE LEAVES OF MANY COLORS ARE FREE TO FLY OR STAY.

SHOULD IT RETURN
1981

I CHERISH THE BEAUTY AND COLOR OF FALL.

I LOVE THE ENCHANTMENT OF THE GOLDEN HUES.

AS I AM ABOUT TO LIFT A TARNISHED LEAF ...
IT SIMPLY BLOWS AWAY.

I WATCHED IT FOR AWHILE ... SWIRLING, GOING NOWHERE,

YET JUST BEYOND MY GRASP.

WHEN I'D GROW NEAR, IT'D BLOW AWAY.

T'WAS LOST AMONG THE OTHERS.

... FROM ME, IT'S GONE AWAY.

AS EVENING SETS, THE WIND DIES DOWN,

THE FULL MOON CASTS IT'S SPELL.

LIKE MAGIC ...

THERE AT MY FEET, THE TARNISHED LEAF

HAD FOUND ITS WAY BACK TO ME.

IN THE CALM OF THE NIGHT, I PICKED IT UP

TO TREASURE FOREVER.

Projection

1981

Sitting in the quiet of the night with a heavy heart ...
Many mixed thoughts and feelings churning deep inside.

There are questions and more questions.
The answers are inadequate or few.

Only that which may be known ...
the black and the white, and all that is grey.

Do I dare to pose the questions?
Who can I trust for the answers?
In the quiet of the night, I will seek out the truth.

A Summer Thought

1983

I need to be

At a place by the sea ...

To set my mind and my spirit free.

The Coming of Spring

1981

The coldness of a long winter
melted under warm rays of sun.
A single blossom bloomed, opening its arms
to embrace the beauty of the day.

Oh! What glory in that newfound goodness
that had once been chilled and dormant
Until ...
Slowly, very slowly the coaxing of the sun,
indeed, accomplished its task.

Untimely came again the tinge of frost.
Yet, strangely, that blossom still bloomed,
drawing from the rays absorbed,
withstood the adversity
and ...
springtime came again.

Awaken to Life

1981

Silently I sit in the early morning darkness.
Loneliness overcomes me,

like the fog rolling in from the sea.
Softly, gently, I allow it to engulf me
so I am no longer aware of the beauty about me.

Slowly, depression creeps into my being, eating away at my soul.

And I wallow in it ... wondering – Why? How?
Savoring every minute of this self-punishment.

For hours I exist ... dwelling on that which I cannot alter.
Pondering, pondering what is ...

From sheer exhaustion my thoughts slowly, unknowingly,

shift to the sun rising over the distant mountains.

From my balcony I breathe in the miracle of a new day ... a new hope.

I marvel at the far off hills and foliage
and all the beauty surrounding me.

And I feel ashamed ...

For I have been granted another day to drink in all
that is good and wonderful.

I feel warm and awake inside, for I have much.

Many resources to tap from within and much to enjoy.

I know that God did not grant me this day to indulge in self-pity.

For each road that is blocked, another unfolds, opening
new pathways and broadening horizons,

waiting for me to reach out and grasp.

Though strength can be drawn from those who love me,

I know, as sure as this morning's sun,
that it is I who must take that first step.

And then, one step at a time,
throughout each day from the path that I have chosen.

As I go surefooted, I will be less anxious.
I will seek out the glories of each day ..

The warmth of those I love ...
the courage to change what I can ... and the will to be happy !

My Dad

1982

How difficult indeed it is to see my Dad

feeble and in need.

It hurts and makes me sad.

No longer is he vain, no longer is he sharp.

He takes his steps in pain,

on ailments does he harp.

He conjures up his "friends", lonely as he is ... 12/30/82

My verse is yet undone, it tears my heart to say.

No more will we have fun,

my Dad has passed away.

With God he is in peace, his voyage now is made.

And when his strife did cease,

me and my "Bro" ...

we closed his eyes and prayed.

My Father's Hands

1982

The lines are well defined within my Father's hands.

They tell of time and toil endured
throughout the years.

My Father's hands
designed for "fix'n" all my things,

grow weary as years pass
but still can quell my fears.

They still reflect his character
and still show signs of strength,

though tremors now prevail,
there's a gentleness that calms.

His help is somewhat different
in support and deep concern.

Those bent, worn hands show love,

there's peace in Daddy's palms.

Art work of hands by Tom o'Conner.

Set to music by Tabitha Booth at Last Rites event.

Copyright - 2019

MY PLAYGROUND

1983

SEE SAW ... SWING ... MERRY-GO-ROUND ... SLIDING BOARD

SEE SAW

SEE SAW, UP AND DOWN.

THERE'S ALWAYS A SMILE AFTER A FROWN!

SWING

IT'S HARD TO PUMP YOURSELF UP WHEN YOU TRY TO SWING ALONE.

WHEN SOMEONE HELPS YOU, IT'S EASY TO SAIL UP IN THE AIR.

WHEN SOMEONE LETS YOU GO, YOU'LL ALWAYS COME BACK HOME.

MERRY-GO-ROUND

HERE WE GO, ROUND AND ROUND, GOING NOWHERE, NOTHING FOUND.

FOR MANY THE CYCLE CONTINUES AS ENDLESS.

THE COURAGEOUS JUMP OFF, THE EXPERIENCE TREMENDOUS.

SLIDING BOARD

I AM DRAWN TO THE SLIDING BOARD LIKE A MAGNET.

THE CLIMB UP THE LADDER IS TOUGH; THE SLIDE DOWN IS FAST.

SOMETIMES THE LANDING IS SPLASHING IN THE WATER.

SOMETIMES I LAND IN THE SAND ...
AND THEN AT TIMES I FEEL THE BRUISE FROM THE PEBBLES BELOW.

YET, NO MATTER WHAT I FIND,
I RUN BACK TO THE SLIDE AND START THE CLIMB AGAIN.

THERE IS MAGIC IN THE SLIDING BOARD!

I DON'T ALWAYS LOOK WHERE I'M BOUND TO LAND.

SOMETIMES I SPLASHED IN THE WATER,
AND NOT OFTEN ENOUGH IN THE SAND.

BUT WHEN I HIT THOSE PEBBLES BELOW,
I TRIED NOT TO DO IT AGAIN!

A Silver Lining

A 25th Anniversary Tribute to my sister, Rose and Mike Rabasca

1982

Good friends and family gather here to celebrate "their" day.

Let us take a moment's pause … reflect upon life's way.

They started out so very young, they fell so much in love.

They overcame adversities with strength from up above.

Those early years they struggled, their goals they did define.

And grim determination reigned as each was reached in time.

They've raised four children with respect,
each unique and proud.

Of course, there was a cat and dog,
plus much "for crying out loud"!

Their love has grown throughout the years,
"togetherness" they have found.

Their life and values intertwined, in love, they do abound.

Whether it be work or friends, in each and every dealing,

They're dedicated and sincere because they're truly caring.

The best of health, the most of wealth
we hope will fill your life,

And that your love will grow
and last forever without strife.

And so, we come to gather here to show love and respect,

For all you've done and who you are,
there's much you can expect.

We wish you joy and happiness and never any pining.

We hope that each,
if any, cloud will have a silver lining.

Know I Understand
1982

I know we each must do what foremost needs our care.

Whatever time it takes, just know that I'll be there.

To hold you and to help you, to listen to your cares.

To love you and to comfort you right now and through
the years.

No longer do I feel that fate can block our path,

She carries not such thunder, and I fear not her rath.

She's just life's hills and valleys and not a vengeful force,

'Cause we're life's engineers, we pattern out our course.

We used to meet each valley alone and tough and torn,

We've grown so close together, let's share each heavy
storm.

For rough times can be eased by knowing each are there ...

And somehow, we'll survive, because we really care.

I've never felt such happiness, our love has truly grown.

I feel we share a fantasy ... each other for our own.

We have the deepest empathy for what we each must bear.

We also have the greatest love that any two can share.

AFTER I'M GONE

1982

I WANT TO BE ONE WITH THE SEA AND THE EARTH,

I WANT NO PART OF A DIRGE.

WHAT A JOY TO BE PART OF THE GRASS AND THE TREES,

TO BE PART OF THE FLOWERS AND BEES.

MY SPIRIT IS FREE AND MUST REMAIN TO BE,

SO LET ME FLY FREE ON THE EARTH AND SEA.

THEN I WILL STILL "BE" WHEN I FALL TO THE GROUND ...

IF YOU'LL SCATTER MY ASHES AROUND.

RIPPLES IN THE SEA

1982

I WATCH EACH WAVE AS IT RUSHES ONTO THE SHORE,

THERE SEEMS TO BE NO END ...

EACH WAVE IS AS VIBRANT AND PURPOSEFUL AS THE NEXT.

I WATCH THEM SWELL AND TAPER ... AND KNOW THERE IS NO END.

FOR EACH, IN TURN, IS SWALLOWED UP BY THE SEA
AND CHURNED INTO A NEW BEGINNING.

I SEE NO END TO THE SEA ...

I WATCH EACH WAVE AS IT RUSHES ONTO THE SHORE ...

AS MY THOUGHT DEEPENS, I AM STRUCK WITH A PARALLEL ...

I 'LIVE" BECAUSE I AM AS ENDLESS AS THE SEA
WITH A LIFE OF VIBRANCE AND PURPOSE.

AND WHEN MY TIME IS DONE, I WILL NOT BE GONE ...

I WILL BE CAUGHT UP IN A NEW BEGINNING.

MY FORCE STILL WILL "BE"...

AS TIMELESS AS THE RIPPLES IN THE SEA.

A Moment of Peace

1983

A sweet serenity pervades this scenic beauty.

The crisp blueness of the sky spotted with cirrus ...

And beneath it all, canoes moved swiftly down river

with the rushing current of the stream.

As if I could pluck a puffy cloud
and touch the mountain rim ...

I gaze at the varied lush of green.

Silently I sit swimming with an awareness

of an inner peace that swells within my soul ...

in this place of scenic beauty.

Drifting Off

1983

Lush green trees framed against the blue sky.

Winds blow, birds fly ...

clouds form, thoughts wander ...

No scene could be fonder.

Restless Sea

1983

The restless white caps surface
as they await their turnto rush onto the shore.

As far as the horizon, they are impatient
to reach their destination.

In time, their turn does come.

They peak and taper gently, settling onto the shore.

Inside I feel so restless, for as if those caps were me,

I know my calm will come

as did the turmoiled sea.

Perfect? Not I

1984

If I were perfect, I would be

a plastic doll in a case to see.

But I feel hurt, and I feel pain,

and may get feisty in times of strain.

Sometimes I laugh, and there are times I cry, too.

And sometimes my sarcasm makes one blue.

But always know that deep inside,

there is fondness for all those to whom I chide.

GRIEF

1983

I REACH FOR CONSOLATION IN MY LOSS ...

TO EASE THE HURT INSIDE ... TO BRIDGE THE VOID WITHIN ...

A NEED TO FEEL THERE IS SOMEONE THERE WHO CARES,
WHO REALLY UNDERSTANDS.

MY DAD ...

HE ALWAYS UNDERSTOOD
WITHOUT A NEED TO KNOW THE PROBLEM.

HE ALWAYS EASED MY BURDEN, ALWAYS SHOWED HE CARED.

HE LEFT ME NEEDING HIM STILL ...

I AM ANGERED THAT MY DAD HAS PASSED AWAY.

FILLED WITH DREADFUL WONDER
IF I COULD HAVE DONE SOMETHING MORE ...

I AM GRASPING FOR HIS COMFORT THAT IS THERE NO MORE.

GROPING FOR SOMEONE TO FILL HIS SHOES,
YET, KNOWING IT CANNOT BE DONE.

WHO WILL BE THERE TO GIVE ME THE COURAGE
TO MOVE INTO THAT NEXT PLATEAU OF LIFE?

SO VERY UNPREPARED, TRYING TO UNDERSTAND,
TRYING TO SORT IT ALL OUT ...

TO FIND THE SOLACE DEEP WITHIN TO ACCEPT

THAT HE IS TRULY GONE FROM ME,

AS I CONTINUE ON,

TO MINE OWN ANCHOR BE ...

My Wish
1984

If only I could openly share ...
my deepest thoughts and feelings ...
to neither be judged nor admonished,
but to be loved for who I am.
As my thoughts are simply thoughts
I need to air ...
to be accepted and respected.

That Rose Along the Way

1984

I WONDER, SHOULD I'VE PICKED THAT ROSE
I LEFT ALONG THE WAY?

IT SADDENED ME WHEN I FOUND OUT
WHAT I KNEW NOT THAT DAY.

A ROSE PROTECTED BY ITS THORNS NEEDS CARE SO IT CAN GROW.

I FEARED TO TOUCH THE THORNS ON IT,
FOR HURT IT WOULD BESTOW.

THE ROSE THAT BLOSSOMED THROUGH THE YEARS
GREW THORNS THAT TRULY SMART.

PER CHANCE ONE DAY IT FOUND ITS WAY
RIGHT BACK INTO MY HEART.

THAT DAY OUR PATHS DID CROSS ONCE MORE,
T'WAS AS WE DID NOT PART.

WHEN I REACHED THROUGH TO TOUCH THAT ROSE,
ITS THORNS I STILL DID FEAR.

ALTHOUGH IT WANTS THAT LOVING CARE,
ITS THORNS SAY DON'T COME NEAR.

AS I STEP BACK EACH TIME I HURT, I WANT TO RUN AWAY,

BUT WHEN I THINK OF ALL ITS JOY, I KNOW I WANT TO STAY.

I NOTICED, YET, AS TIME DOES PASS,
SOME THORNS DROP OFF EACH DAY.

I WONDER, SHALL I KEEP THAT ROSE ONCE LEFT ALONG THE WAY?

SOMETIMES IN THE SUN ...

1984

I LOVE TO STRETCH OUT IN THE WARM SUMMER SUN.

AT FIRST, I AM ONLY AWARE OF THE PLAYFUL CHIRP OF THE BIRDS.

THEN, I FEEL A COOLING BREEZE BRUSH ACROSS MY TANNING BODY.

I OPEN MY EYES AND DRINK IN THE CRYSTAL BLUE SKY.

THE LUSH GREEN TREES SWAY GENTLY IN THE BREEZE.

SOMETIMES, IN THE DISTANCE,

I LISTEN TO THE DRONE OF A PLANE ...

MINDFUL OF DAYS LONG GONE.

GAZING AT THE SHAPES OF CLOUDS,

DREAMING OF THINGS I'D DO ...

COMFORTABLE IN MY REFLECTIONS,

I ENJOY THE COOLING WATER SPRAY,

AND SLIP AWAY INTO DREAMS OF ALL THE HAPPY TIMES ...

SO SAFE AND SO SECURE IN THE SUMMER SUN.

... THEN OTHER TIMES IN THE SUN

I FELT THE SILENT BREEZE

AND LISTENED TO THE SWEET TRILL OF A LARK.

STRETCHED LONG AND LANKY AND BROWN AS A BARK,

I LAY BASKING IN THE SUN, IT SEEMED, WITHOUT A CARE.

MY THOUGHTS FLOWED FREELY, DREDGING UP ALL THAT I FEAR.

I FEEL THE TEARS TRICKLE SLOWLY DOWN MY CHEEK,

AS I ALLOW MYSELF TO BE ENVELOPED
BY THE ANSWERS THAT I SEEK ...

A WAY TO GO

1984

Reach for love. It lies just beyond.

Reach for life 'fore it slips slowly away.

Enjoy the laughter, it brightens the spirit.

Seek out happiness …

It is the spirit brightened.

ROCKY ROADS
1984

MANY ROADS ARE ROCKY AND ROUGH.

ENDLESS WINDING, MUCH TO DODGE.

GROWING WEARY, MUST GET TOUGH.

A CRYSTAL LAKE?

NO, A MIRAGE.

To Share a Moment

1984

To share a thought, a feeling, a dream ...

To laugh, to love, to scheme.

Smell a rose, crunch a twig, feel a breeze,

or watch the waves at shoreline tease ...

is to live!

BEND IN THE WIND

1984

BEND IN THE WIND,

DRAW STRENGTH FROM THE SUN,

AND ONE CAN WEATHER THE STORM.

CLIMB UP THAT MOUNT,

KEEP A SURE, STEADY GAIT,

AND 'FORE LONG YOU WILL CONQUER THAT GIANT.

ALONENESS

1984

I FEEL A JOYFUL ALONENESS ...

THAT IS MY CHOICE TONIGHT.

A PEACEFUL TIME TO THINK ...

TO REFLECT ON THE "NOW",

TO DECIDE ON THE "WHAT" AND THE "WHEN".

A WELCOMED ALONENESS ...

A QUIET, PEACEFUL REFURBISHMENT.

THE FORCE

1985

Such force within the skies ...
it reaches deep within.
Spatial journey binds the ties ...
the danger lies there in.

A prophecy fulfilled ...
take heed of what will be.
One precious love destroyed
in my house of Mercury.

A struggle to be master
of fates that lie ahead,
'tween stars that speed on faster
and the goals for which I've bled.

A Search For Life
1985

So long have I sought the meaning to life ...
to love ... to happiness ...

And as I've searched, so much has slipped me by.
I dwelled on the past and awaited the future ...

But today lived well I have found...
To give joy to those you love - today.
Meet challenges - today.

And at day's end give a smile of sweet content
for another day well spent.

MY SON

1985

I THANK THE LORD FOR ALL I HAVE.
HE MADE ME STRONG AND SMART.

THEN, UPON ME HE DID BESTOW
A SON TO STEAL MY HEART.

I WORKED TO MAKE HIM STRONG
AND WISE IN BODY AND IN MIND.

HE IS MY ONE AND ONLY, A
ND IS ONE OF A KIND!

HE'S SALTY AND HE'S STRONG OF WILL,
HE'S TALENTED AND BRIGHT.

HE SHOWS CONCERN, INTEGRITY
AND STANDS BY WHAT IS RIGHT.

I'VE SEEN HIM GROW THROUGH ALL THESE YEARS,
HE'LL BE 18 IN DAYS,

THROUGH ALL THE TRIALS AS HE DID GROW,
"I LOVE YOU MOM" HE'D SAY.

NO LONGER IS HE "MY LITTLE BOY" ...

A BRIGHT YOUNG MAN IS HE!

I SEE A SON OF WHOM I'M PROUD ...

THE DEAREST PART OF ME.

FREEDOM'S DOOR

1986

TO STAND UP TALL, TO STAND UP FREE,

IS WHAT "THE LADY" MEANS TO ME.

THERE IS NO FEAR, THERE IS NO DOUBT,

"THE LADY" STANDS FOR FREEDOM'S CLOUT.

PROTECT THE TORCH, PROTECT THE CROWN,

"THE LADY" WILL BE NE'ER LET DOWN.

THOUGH LANDS BE FAR, THOUGH LANDS BE NEAR,

THE FREEDOM "SYMBOL" CUTS THROUGH CLEAR.

SO COME YE TIRED,

COME YE POOR

COME TO KNOCK

ON FREEDOM'S DOOR.

With Your Love

1987

Take my hand, my loved one ...
lead me through the haze ...

From time to time I'll tarry
within the jumbled maze.

Touch my soul, my loved one,
remove that seed of doubt ...

This could be the love I seek
yet, fear its forceful clout.

My Southern Gentleman

1987

He whispers words I love to hear,

and showers me with flowers.

He says he truly knows me,

as he shares my joys and sorrows.

He makes me happy as can be

and tells me this is destiny.

I Am There

1987

I SEND YOU THE WIND …

IT WHISPERS "I LOVE YOU".

I SEND YOU THE COLD …

TO REMEMBER OUR WARMTH.

I SEND YOU THE SPRINGTIME …

AS OUR LOVE WILL BLOSSOM.

I SEND YOU MY LOVE,

SO YOU WILL NEVER BE LONESOME.

FINALLY FREE

1987

IT CAUSED AN ANXIOUS FEELING TO BE TRAPPED
AND YET, SO FREE ...

TO WANT A TRUE AND LASTING LOVE, YET,
THIS ONE CANNOT BE.

THE EMPATHY OF THIS ONE LOVE, WOULD LEAD ME TO THE DOOR,

WHY COULD I NOT IN HONESTY LOVE "ONE" FOREVER MORE?

FROM HER MICROSCOPE OF SCRUTINY,
SHE HELPED ME STRUGGLE FREE.

HIS LOVE AND UNDERSTANDING
WAS THE BEAM OF LIGHT FOR ME.

HE STOOD WITH HAND AND HEART OUTSTRETCHED,

WITH LOVE HE WATCHED MY FLY ...

AND THEN I FELT THE MOTH INSIDE

BECOME A BUTTERFLY.

My Shoes
1996

My shoes are near and dear to me, especially on my toes.
They hang out in my closet, as company for my clothes.

I have shoes of every color; I have shoes of every kind.
They are many shapes and sizes in my closet you will find.

I have pointed toes and rounded toes,
and heels so high and low.
Some are shiny, some are scruffy,
some have laces or Velcro.

Some I got while traveling far,
and some I got 'round here.

Each has its special story with a secret, I do fear!

A Perfect Love
2000

If there were a symbol of our love, it would be a rose.
In its beauty and perfection, at a point in time it froze.

There are no words that could express
our wondrous love or why.

Not the depth and breadth of the ocean
nor the height of stars in the sky.

Too soon he left as he "passed on" as suddenly as we met.
The depth of sorrow in my heart burns deeply as of yet.

In grief I roamed to places, our treasured moments spent ...
There my restless spirit quelled
with words of love he'd meant.

He said I'd filled a chasm vast,
he'd searched for many years.

We filled our hearts and souls with love,

His spirit ... now dries my tears.

MOTHER

2002

MOTHER ...

A WORD, A PERSON, A LIFELINE.

ONE WHOM I'VE OFTEN TAKEN FOR GRANTED,

VERBALLY ABUSED, AND EVEN DISREGARDED ...

BECAUSE, AFTER ALL, "I" KNEW BETTER.

UNTIL ....

ONE DAY I CAME TO REALIZE
THE VALUE OF HAVING MOTHER THERE.

ALWAYS TO BE COUNTED UPON,
ESPECIALLY WHEN TIMES WERE TOUGH.

ALWAYS THERE TO UNDERSTAND
WHEN NO ONE ELSE REALLY CARED.

HER EYES GREW SAD
AS THEY SUFFERED MY SORROWS AND DARK DAYS.

"IT'S ALRIGHT" SHE'D SAY, "JUST HAVE FAITH".

A TOUCH OF HER SOFT, GENTLE HANDS
SAID "I DON'T WANT YOU TO HURT".

HER LOVING HUG SAID "BE STRONG"
AND WAS A COMFORT TO ME.

AND THEN, ONE SAD NIGHT, SHE PASSED AWAY ...

MOTHER WAS GONE.

A PERSON, A LIFELINE ... MY ANCHOR ...

HER LESSONS LEFT BEHIND.

My Prince

2005

Once upon a time, it came to be you found me ...

you entered my life to become my worthy friend,

who brought caring and laughter to my life.

You took my hand and brought honesty and trust
to our love.

You crept into each carefully guarded crevice of my
heart

and brought happiness and a smile to my being ...

For these things, I love you.

Together we live happily to enjoy today

and our journey towards each tomorrow.

His Passage ...

2015

His tears streamed down his cheeks;
he had not long to live.

He said to me, "do not be sad",
but tears were all we had.

He repeated how he loved me;
I had no words to say.

We sat there unbelieving;
what fate had thrown our way.

I held his hand all through the night,

and kissed him now and then.

I know he knew that I was there,

he squeezed my hand in fear.

His children came at 10:00 am, and said to go away.

So off I went to work again and there I spent the day.

I headed back to him that night in hopes to sit and pray.

I got the call en route to say ...

my love had passed away.

... And Then He Was Gone
2015

I treasure the moments and laughter we shared.

In a week he was gone, we were so unprepared.

My heart is so empty ... with sadness I cry.

My soulmate crossed over without my goodbye.

Where is your soul? Where are you, my love?

So suddenly gone, flew away like a dove.

It's hard here without you, you're always in mind.

'Cause we vowed we'd grow old with the love we did find.

Ms. Corona Virus
2020

Ms. Corona Virus came to the USA.
She came to us from "Somewhere",
and here she chose to stay.

She ravished many bodies, and rattled in our mind,
our lives went topsy-turvy, relief was hard to find.

As she sat and surveyed damage on a temporary rest,
she smiled and thought she could do more
to reach her venom best.

So back she came with vengeance,
what were we all to do?
So unprepared were we to cope, to deal with all the "poo"!

We got upon our feet again, we could not bear defeat!
We struggled hard, we struggled long,
the foe we soon would meet.

We saw that she was weakened as we struck with all our
might.
We saw that we could overcome,

if each did what was right !

Is Love Elusive?

2020

Love seems elusive, I wish that it would stay.
So often its joy just quickly slips away.

It draws me to wonder ... can one truly find
what could only be briefly, a state of the mind?

I see love can be found in many forms ...
in the trees, and the sky and even in a storm.
Such treasures are there should one look so deep.
Know THAT kind of love is forever to keep.

My 'Lil Nynja

2020

There is a 'Lil Nynja,
she is so strong and smart.

She loves to gather people, inspiration to impart.

She is sweet and energetic, she loves to find a challenge,

I have no doubt she will prevail
to meet her goals and manage.

I noticed like a rising star,
she struggled to shine bright.

It matters not if near or far,
she'll fight for what is right.

Her smile is so engaging,
there's s sparkle in her eyes,

it shows determination
to succeed in what she tries.

My Friend, My Sister

2020

I found a true and trusting friend,
so sweet and nice is she.

Always there with a willing hand,
as helpful as can be.

At times when things seemed awfully blue,
she gave me consolation.

Her understanding air rang true
to give me motivation.

Birds of Many Colors

2020

What a wonderful sight to see so many birds in flight.

They flutter here and flutter there
and rest within our sight.

We see their many colors and hear their many sounds.

Their feathers catch our eyes,
you see, such beauty does abound.

Among them are red robins,
the bluebirds and brown sparrows.

We watch them settle in to play,
their difference truly narrows.

Together all the colors blend,
it brings joy to our heart,

and as we watch, they all fly free,
together from the start.

THE RIVER
2020

THE RUSHING WATERS TUMBLED DOWN
THE HILL OF ROCKS AND BOULDERS.
WE SAT AND WONDERED ...
COULD IT BE LIKE ANGER ON OUR SHOULDERS?

SOON THE PEACEFUL WATERS FLOWED
WHICH ADDED TO THE CALM.
AS WE LOOKED DOWN TO GIVE A SIGH,
PEACE SETTLED IN OUR PALM.

Joy of a Storm

2020

In the dead of the night, the sky lit up,

the lightening frightened me.

The thunder came and then the rain ...

it poured relentlessly.

As that great storm did plummet us,

this time we were prepared.

We watched the lightening show above,

a bright sight we all shared.

Nature likens unto life

when causing devastation.

Our secret is the sun will shine ...

it's part of our creation.

Lightning Source UK Ltd.
Milton Keynes UK
UKHW040739051222
413416UK00001B/121